Choosing Is Confusing

How to Make Good Choices, Not Bad Guesses

Claudine G. Wirths & Mary Bowman-Kruhm

Illustrations by Ed Taber

CPP BOOKS
Palo Alto, California
A Division of Consulting Psychologists Press, Inc.

Also in this same series by these authors:
Are You My Type, Or Why Aren't You More Like Me?
Upgrade: How to Boot Up Your Grades With High Tech

Copyright 1994 by Consulting Psychologists Press, Inc., 3803 E. Bayshore Road, Palo Alto, CA 94303. All rights reserved. No part of this book may be reproduced, stored in a retrieval system, or transmitted in any form or by any means, electrical, mechanical, photocopying, recording, or otherwise, without written permission of the Publisher.

98 97 96 95 94   10 9 8 7 6 5 4 3 2 1
Printed in the United States of America

Library of Congress Cataloging-in-Publication Data
Wirths, Claudine G.
    Choosing is confusing : how to make good choices, not bad guesses /
    Claudine G. Wirths, Mary Bowman-Kruhm : illustrations by Ed Taber.
        p.   cm.
    ISBN 0-89106-068-5
    1. Decision-making—Juvenile literature.   2. Choice (Psychology)—
Juvenile literature.   [1. Decision-making.   2. Choice.]
I. Bowman-Kruhm, Mary.   II. Taber, Ed, ill.   III. Title.
BF448.W57 1994
153.8'3—dc20   94-17751
                                                             CIP
                                                              AC

First edition
        First printing 1994

To our fathers,
Count D. Gibson and Bradley L. Bowman,
who encouraged us to make choices that were
not easy or traditional ones.
And to all the young people who read this book,
with the hope that they, too,
will be encouraged to make these kinds of
choices.

About the Authors

Claudine G. Wirths has a master's degree in psychology and another in special education. She has been a police psychologist and consultant in environmental decision making as well as an educator and member of the adjunct faculty of Frederick Community College in Maryland. She is now a full-time consultant, speaker, and freelance writer.

Mary Bowman-Kruhm has a doctorate in education. She was a teacher and administrator with Montgomery County Public Schools in Maryland in regular and special education and has taught at the University of Maryland and Western Maryland College. She is now a full-time freelance writer and consultant/speaker and has never regretted her career choice to work with young people. She does, however, admit to having made some bad choices in other areas of her life, all of which she now considers good preparation for writing this book.

Also in this same series by these authors are *Are You My Type, or Why Aren't You More Like Me?* and *Upgrade: How to Boot Up Your Grades With High Tech.*

Contents

Contents

Introduction

"Let me pick what *I* want. Puh-leeese!"

"Gee, you mean it's up to me?"

"I hate it when you make me decide."

Sound familiar? Sometimes you want to be the one to choose. Sometimes you don't. Sometimes you aren't sure *what* you want.

As you've grown up, making choices has grown harder. When you were little, your life was pretty simple. Your parents chose what you ate, what you wore, and how you spent your time. Now that you're getting older, your life is getting more complicated and so are the choices facing you. Choosing can be confusing.

What and how you choose depends a lot on who you are and what is important to you. But keep in mind that the choices you make—big and little—do matter. Making the right ones can give you a sense of power, a feeling that, as you get older, you are beginning to take charge of your own life.

In this book, we'll help you learn to make good choices, not bad guesses. We'll talk about the kinds of choices you have and how to make ones that are right for you. We'll tell you how your choices affect others and what to do if you change your mind about a choice you've made. We'll even give you some tips on how to get parents and teachers to change their minds if their choice is different from what you choose!

Sound interesting? Then read on while we talk about making choices with another young person, someone a lot like you.

1

Choosing to Choose

Teacher:	Your group has five minutes to choose a topic for your report on China.
Amber:	I think we should report on the Great Wall.
Michael:	I'd rather pick that army the teacher talked about that's made out of stone.
Ali:	I want to do our report on Chinese food. We could even bring some in for everyone to taste. But the terra-cotta army is my second choice.
You:	I'll go along with whatever all of you pick.

Welcome to the mixed-up world of being a teen. One minute your parents say you're old enough to get home on time, the next minute they say you're too young to decide when to go to bed! Teachers ask you to pick your own science project but won't let you decide when to go to the restroom.

You've got that right! Why do adults act that way?

Adults are not sure what choices you can be trusted to make because you are growing and changing so fast. They want to let you grow up, but since you haven't had much experience in making choices yet, they're afraid that you'll make poor ones.

Mostly my parents and teachers let me pick from choices they've already made. They say, "Do you want this or do you want that?"

Limiting your choices is one way to help you avoid making poor ones. Parents and teachers also want to be sure that once you start making choices on your own, you'll know what kinds of choices they think are good.

Making your own choices is an important skill for you to learn because it gives you more control over your life as you grow up. And because it is like any other skill, you *can* learn how to make good choices. This book will help you.

Even when I have choices I can make, sometimes I don't make them. I can't figure out why I do that.

Everyone worries about making choices—some people worry a little, others worry a lot—but each of us feels concerned for very different reasons. Some people have been told that trying to get their own way is not good manners. They may act so polite that they elect not to be the one to choose when a choice is offered.

Other people are afraid of making mistakes. They don't realize that mistakes are part of learning, and they should not be overly concerned about making them. Others worry about losing friends if they don't choose the same things their friends like. They don't understand that real friends want people to be themselves. Still others don't want to make a choice because they don't want to take responsibility for what happens when they choose, so they try to get someone else to choose for them.

If I don't want to make a choice, I always get someone else to choose for me.

Did you ever stop to think that when you let someone else choose for you that you are still making a choice and that you are still responsible for it?

Rewind that tape! Are you telling me that I'm to blame for making a choice when someone else makes it for me and I don't say or do anything?

Exactly! When you have a choice to make and you don't make it, you are choosing to leave the choice to someone else.

But I *have* to let other people make choices for me sometimes. I can't choose where I live—my parents do.

We didn't say that letting someone else choose for you is necessarily a *bad* choice. It can be good or bad. Letting your parents choose where you live at your age is a good choice. You can make that choice yourself by running away, but running away is a bad choice. Staying home from a school play because the doctor said you should is also a good choice.

More and more times in your teens, you will be deciding whether to choose for yourself or to choose to let someone else choose for you. If you knowingly let someone else choose for you, then you should be aware that you are responsible for that choice and what happens because of it.

My friends and I choose for each other all the time. You know—where to hang out, what movie to see. If a friend makes a bad choice of a movie, I don't blame myself—or my friend either, for that matter.

But choosing what movie to see is a fairly easy decision to make. What if some people try to make an *important* decision for you? Suppose they tell you that, if you want to be friends with them, you have to smoke. Then remind yourself that no matter how hard you are pressured, the choice is always *yours*. You wouldn't be able to blame anyone else if you got hooked on nicotine because you would have made the choice to smoke yourself, regardless of whether it was your idea.

But that's a *big* decision. I don't see what's wrong with going along with my friends about small stuff.

Oh, you're right; there's nothing wrong with that. If you are talking about little decisions that are easy to make, it often doesn't matter if you or someone else makes them. Tomorrow you won't care about those choices. In this book, we call that kind of choice **E** for easy.

I wish my parents would let me make E choices more often.

Oh, but they do. You already make more than 500 E choices every day. Every time you have several ways of doing something, you make an E choice. You choose when it's safe to cross the street, what to tape on your notebook, how to comb your hair—things like that. You don't think of them as choices because you make most of them while you're on automatic pilot, but they are choices all the same.

Like what socks to wear today?

Good example. By next week, no one, not even you, is likely to remember which ones you decided to wear.

What about tougher choices?

Many choices *are* tougher and not so easy to make. One choice may not be clearly better than another. Or you may know that whatever you choose, you'll be stuck with that choice for a while. We call these choices **M** for middle-sized. M choices are ones that cause you to say, "Mmm," and to think before you decide. Imagine yourself pacing back and forth and saying, "Mmm-mm. What should I do?" and you'll see why we call them M choices. Buying a pair of boots is a good example of an M choice. Because you want a pair that looks right and feels right, ones you'll be happy wearing for a long time, you need to take some time to consider your options—the price, style, and comfort of the boots, for instance.

Would it also be an M choice if one of my friends wants me to go to the movies and another friend wants me to go to the mall?

Yes. Although you would no doubt like to do both, choosing the wrong thing to do and say could hurt one of your friends. So you have to think awhile before you decide.

Those M choices can be hard to make.

But not as hard as others we call **H** for hard, very hard choices that matter a lot in your life. For example, suppose the parents of one of your friends divorce and your friend has to pick which parent to live with. That would be an H choice—a very hard choice to make and one that will affect not only your friend but other people in his life for a long time. He needs to make that decision for himself, however hard it is to make.

I wish all choices were E ones.

Most choices are. So don't go through life worrying about every choice you make. Save your energy for the ones that really matter, the M and H ones. Making a poor M or H choice can truly add to your problems.

> ▶ *Take a few moments now to look at the exercise on the next page and consider some of the choices you know you'll be making within the next month—everything from everyday choices like what books you want to read to more difficult ones like how you'd like to spend your summer vacation. After you've listed your choices, then rate them according to what kind of choices they are—E for easy, M for middle-sized, and H for hard. Then we'll talk some more about the different kinds of choices there are.*

Last year I thought I made a good choice, but I ended up with a problem anyway. When two friends decided to let the air out of a teacher's tire, I chose just to watch them. Didn't I make an M choice?

For sure an M and maybe an H.

Choices You Expect to Make Within the Next Month

1.

Will it be an E, M, or H choice? ❏ E ❏ M ❏ H

2.

Will it be an E, M, or H choice? ❏ E ❏ M ❏ H

3.

Will it be an E, M, or H choice? ❏ E ❏ M ❏ H

4.

Will it be an E, M, or H choice? ❏ E ❏ M ❏ H

5.

Will it be an E, M, or H choice? ❏ E ❏ M ❏ H

But the principal recognized me and not the two kids who did it, so I was punished. That didn't seem fair. My friends chose to hurt the teacher, not me.

But the choice you made to stay and watch was not a wise one.

I chose *not* to let the air out of the tire. Should I have chosen to go along with the kids who did it?

We are definitely not telling you that! But we are saying that choosing can get pretty complicated and confusing. You had several other choices you could have made. You could have tried to get the kids not to do it, or walked away when you knew what they were up to, or told on them. As it was, you chose to stay around and watch them do something wrong. The law calls that being an "accessory" to an act. Our laws say that as an accessory you are partly responsible and that you have to accept part of the blame because you hung around and didn't tell on them.

I don't believe in squealing on other kids.

If you didn't want to be blamed, you shouldn't have made the choice you did. Remember: *You always have choices and you are always responsible for what you say, how you act, and where you go.* You can't blame others when you go along with their bad choices—even if you only *seem* to go along with their choices.

Gee, there's a lot more to this choice stuff than I ever thought about before.

That's right. Now let's talk more about why people make the choices they do.

2

Using Values to Choose

Grandma: Celebrating my birthday by bringing me to this beautiful restaurant for dinner was such a lovely thing to do. What are all of you getting? I'll let you order for me.

Mom: Well, I always have the Chicken Paprika. It's so good that I hate to risk trying anything new.

Dad: Where's that waiter? Why does he think we need so much time to make a choice? I decided on Shrimp with Pepper Rice long ago.

Your aunt: Why are you in such a rush? I want to be sure I order just the right thing. Let's see.... I think I'll ask the waiter if the fish has been frozen and then thawed. But maybe if the chicken is broiled without butter, that would be better for me.... Hmm-mm.

You: And I thought eating out was an E choice!

Whether it is an easy, middle-sized, or hard choice, most of us decide based on what we value.

I'm not sure what you mean by *value.*

If you value something, you feel it is important. For example, if you love your family very much, then love of family is one of your values.

You would choose to stand up for your little brother at school if a bully were picking on him, even if you sometimes get really mad at him at home.

Our values, or ideas of what is important, come from two places deep inside us. One of these is what we have learned. The other is our temperament.

Do you mean I make choices because of what I learn in school?

What you learn in school helps you make choices, but what you learn at home and in life outside of school plays a bigger part in the choices you make. From your earliest days, your parents try to teach you what is important to them as a family, or as members of a religion, or as part of a community, or even just as individuals.

Your parents say things like:

- "Our family doesn't do that."

- "Our religion believes that this is important."

- "Who cares about that?"

- "You made me feel proud when you acted that way."

From statements like these, you learn what your parents value. As you get older, you have experiences of your own, outside of your family. You take in these bits of life and store them in your memory. All these life experiences from your home, school, neighborhood, and community combine to help you develop your own sense of values, your sense of what is right and wrong, and what is important to you. Some of your values may change as you have new experiences.

I don't see how my values can change.

Suppose you have a friend who doesn't believe in eating meat. Although you don't miss the meat when you eat at your friend's house, you eat it at home because your mom thinks meat is an important part of a person's diet. If you become very close to your friend and the two of you talk about health and diet and the rights of animals, you may someday make a decision not to eat meat at all. What you learned to value at home changed because of an experience you had outside of your home.

If what we learn by experience is so important in making choices, why does temper-whatever-you-said matter?

Temperament is what we said. Our values come not only from our experiences in life but also from a temperament that seems born in us. When we make a choice, what we say and do often reflects our temperament, the unique behavior pattern that each human being seems to have from the time of birth. Our temperament characteristics help to make us act as we do unless we choose to act otherwise.

My math teacher says a student in our class is temperamental. Is that the same thing?

No. Someone who is high-strung and moody is sometimes called *temperamental*. When we talk about *temperament*, we mean a basic pattern of behavior. People tend to follow their personal pattern of behavior—their temperament type—under almost any conditions. When we make choices, the way that each of us goes about it depends in large part on our temperament.

Last month I was on a committee to buy food for a school party. We argued and argued before we finally agreed what to serve. Could temperament have had anything to do with the trouble we had deciding?

Indeed it could, since temperament influences the choices people prefer. Here are the ways students with the four basic temperament types might look at the problem of choosing the menu for the party:

- "Wait a minute. Before we decide we need to look at what the people who will be there like to eat." In choosing, this person is thinking about how others feel.

- "Let's have the same food we had at the last party." This person is relying on past experiences and traditions in making a choice.

- "Okay, let's choose and get on with it!" This person wants to choose quickly and move on.

- "Hold on. I need to know more." This person likes to make a thoughtful choice.

These people are all using a different way to choose and, because of their temperament, each one probably thinks his or her way is the best way.

There's a great deal more to know about the different temperament types than we can tell you here. If the topic is interesting to you, look up some of the references in the back of this book and read more about temperament. For now, we'll tell you a little about each of the four types and how each makes a choice. Remember, *no one type is any better than the others.*

How do I know which type I am?

When we describe the four temperament types, one of the descriptions will probably make you feel, "Hey! That's me!" Although you may have some traits that belong to each of the four temperament types, you'll find that one is closest to the way you tend to behave most of the time. The words in bold face type are key words to help you remember the different temperament types.

Some kids seem to be super friendly. Are they the ones who would want to know who would be there before they picked the food?

Yes. People who are the first type like other people. As **People Persons**, they look for the best in others and want to get along with everyone. People Persons carefully consider many possibilities, especially what effect their choice will have on others. For the party, they may go along with the soft drinks others want when they would rather have punch.

Does it matter if the choice is an E, M, or H one? I saw this guy on TV who gave up a kidney to help his sister. He sounds like a People Person.

How hard the choice is doesn't matter. The kind of person who makes choices based on a concern for others is a People Person. Their choices are guided by what they feel deep in their hearts is the right thing to do.

But what about the kid who wants the same thing to eat every time?

Someone who is this type is called **Sane-and-Sensible**. Sane-and-Sensibles prefer to look at the facts and make a choice because it is reasonable and smooths out life's snags. If in their view everyone at the party enjoyed pizza and soft drinks before, why spend time and energy planning and fixing new foods that the kids might not like?

That sounds like my cousin. He always wants to go camping at the same place every year. He says that way he knows what to take, what he can buy at the camp store, and even what the showers are like. He got upset when his granddad wanted to go somewhere different.

Since Sane-and-Sensibles like things to march along without problems or change, they often choose what they know works. They like to have a plan and stick to it. The Sane-and-Sensibles of the world dig in, judge the facts, make a choice, and get the job done.

What about the kid who wants to make a choice and move on?

The third type are **Free-and-Fearless** when they have to problem solve or make a decision. With the name Free-and-Fearless, how do you think they tend to choose?

I bet they make quick choices.

Right. The person who is Free-and-Fearless was the one who said, "Okay, let's choose and get on with it!"

Free-and-Fearless are seldom concerned about other people's feelings. They are also often risk takers and impulsive. The Free-and-Fearless may look at the facts, but theirs is a quick glance. They are not as cautious as the Sane-and-Sensibles.

I bet our coach is Free-and-Fearless—he has to make fast choices all the time during a game.

Could be. Someone who is Free-and-Fearless can make a choice and be thinking about what's next while the People Person is still trying to figure out what would satisfy everyone and the Sane-and-Sensible is mulling over facts and figures.

The person who by temperament makes choices quickly is often heroic in an emergency. They may decide M and H problems as quickly as E ones. And they don't look back and kick themselves for making the wrong choice. If the kids at the dance don't like the food, Free-and-Fearless types will just shrug and not worry about it.

And the fourth type?

People who are the fourth type are **Considering-and-Careful** choosers.

I guess they put a lot of thought into a problem before they make a choice.

This would be the person who said, "I need to know more." Sometimes even if the choice is an E one, they take a long time to decide because they feel the need to look at all sides of the problem. Solving it gives them a real sense of success. If this person chooses the food for the dance, they will be happy if no one complains. But if other kids complain, they will be very hard on themselves for choosing the wrong food. They like dealing with ideas and are pleased when they arrive at an answer that is "right."

Do Considering-and-Carefuls pay attention to the facts, like Sane-and-Sensibles?

Considering-and-Careful types don't ignore facts, but they are a lot like People Persons because they also trust a feeling they get in the pit of their stomach to help them make a choice. They are good at reading the feelings and motives of others.

So Considering-and-Careful types choose best?

Remember—we said that no one type is better than another. The style each type tends to use when they choose may be good sometimes and it may not be so good other times. For example, if you have one minute left to finish a test, taking a risk like a Free-and-Fearless type might do could get you a higher grade than analyzing your choices like a Considering-and-Careful type might do.

To help make the different choosing styles of the four types we've been discussing even more recognizable, look at the chart on the next page labeled "How Each Type Chooses." It summarizes what we've talked about and provides an easy reference to type and choosing style. It also makes it easy to compare the four types and their choosing styles.

▶ *Now take a few moments to try your hand at presenting your choices to different types by doing the exercise called "Convincing Others Your Choice Is a Good One." Try to put yourself in the place of the character in the story and, keeping his choice in mind, try and argue for his vacation choice in a way that would appeal to the members of his family and the types you decide they are. Then we'll talk some more about how different types choose.*

How Each Type Chooses

People Person	Sane-and-Sensible	Free-and-Fearless	Considering-and-Careful
• Considers many possibilities	• Tends to make choices that cause little trouble or disruption	• Tends to be impulsive when choosing	• Thinks carefully about the possible choices
• Is concerned about the effect a choice will have on others, regardless of whether it is E, M, or H	• Tends to choose what has been a good choice in the past	• Is willing to make a choice that involves risk taking	• Tends to be independent thinker and often doesn't feel the need to go along with choices of others
• Wants to feel a choice is the right thing to do	• Makes choices that help get a job done	• Focuses on situation at the moment to make a choice	• Is observant of others' feelings and motives when making choices
• Relies more on feelings than facts to make a choice	• Tends to make cautious, practical choices	• Doesn't worry about a poor choice but moves on to other things	• Ultimately relies more on feelings than facts to make a choice
• Feels bad if a choice doesn't seem popular with others or possibly hurts someone else	• Relies more on facts and figures than feelings to make a choice	• May tend not to consider the feelings of others when making a choice	• Feels much personal blame for bad choices
• Has tendency to choose what others want, even if the choice is not in their own best interest			

Convincing Others
Your Choice Is a Good One

Bob's family is planning a weekend trip. Bob suggests going to a vacation theme park. His dad says a trip like that isn't educational, but he doesn't want to over-rule the rest of the family. Bob's mom says a theme park will be very, very expensive and they could go to the beach, where they always go, for much less money. His grandmother says she's heard the park is overrated and the rides aren't safe, but she's willing to still consider it by investigating further. His cousin says, "I'd rather go bungee-jumping." Which of the four temperament types is each of the members of Bob's family? What could Bob say to persuade each one that his choice for the trip is a good one?

Bob's **dad** is a _____ type. To persuade his dad, Bob could use the argument that:	Bob's **mom** is a _____ type. To persuade his mom, Bob could use the argument that:
Bob's **grandmother** is a _____ type. To persuade his grandmother, Bob could use the argument that:	Bob's **cousin** is a _____ type. To persuade his cousin, Bob could use the argument that:

I've got a pretty good idea what type I am. Will I always make a choice based on my type?

Not always. Sometimes you may realize that making a good choice might mean choosing in a way that doesn't come naturally to you. If you understand your type, you can see the strengths—and the weaknesses—of how and why you tend to make decisions the way you do. If you see that making choices as you usually do is not in your best interest, you can push yourself to make choices in a way that will be most helpful to you in a given situation.

I'm not sure I see what you mean.

Let's say you're a Free-and-Fearless type. An oral report has been assigned by your teacher. This is an M problem, because the report is going to count heavily toward your grade for the term. Deciding when and how to get to the library, do the research, and plan what you will talk about are usually big problems for most Free-and-Fearless types. Free-and-Fearless types don't like to plan ahead or plug slowly away on most projects, especially ones that aren't super interesting. Wouldn't you do better if you looked at some of the characteristics of the other types of people and made choices the way they usually do? You'd choose a topic carefully, like a Considering-and-Careful type. You might decide to talk to the librarian and other people who could help you, like a People Person type. Instead of waiting until the night before the report is due, you would plan ahead and start your paper early, like a Sane-and-Sensible type. Then, of course, you would choose to stand in front of the entire class and present your report in the breezy style that comes naturally to your type.

No wonder choosing gets confusing!

It certainly does. Let's talk about how you can make good choices.

3

Choosing How to Make a Choice

You
(to yourself):

I really want a dog. I'll name him Boomer. Now how can I convince my mom? Maybe I can get her to go by the Humane Society, just to look at the dogs, of course. Nah, she'd suspect what I was up to. Or I could get Mark to bring his puppy over to visit. No, it might wet on our new carpet. I could tell her if I can't have a dog for my birthday, I don't want anything. But then I might not get anything. Geez, how can I prove to her that I really, *really* should have a puppy?

No matter what your temperament type, you use four main ways to make choices. Each way is useful sometimes and not useful other times. Here are the four basic ways you choose:

- You choose what you think others want you to choose.

- You choose what you've always chosen.

- You decide quickly and catch the moment.

- You check out facts and feelings and picture the possibilities.

When would it ever be useful to choose what others want?

Choosing what others want is often a choice that helps you get along with others. If everyone wants to go to the ball game and you want to go to the movies, choosing to go with them is the friendly thing to do. When you are with a friend who is a guest in your home, you are polite if you let the other person make E choices, such as what videos you'll watch.

But going along with others is not useful if you go through life never trusting your own values and always choosing what you think would please others, especially in M and H choices. People Persons are especially likely to make the choice others want them to make, even when it isn't in their best interest. The older you get, the less often M or H choices should be made by choosing what others want you to choose. If you choose only what others want you to choose, you are not taking your own values, your family's values, and your type into account, and you may end up feeling uncomfortable about your choice.

Lots of the time, I just choose what I've always chosen.

Putting some of your choices on automatic pilot is the second way of choosing. Doing what you've done in the past is a perfectly good way to make E choices. When you are sleepy in the morning, following a daily routine or set of habits is often the easiest and best way to get going. Your parents have probably established a morning routine for you that fits your family's life patterns.

So habit is how most people make E choices?

Not everyone, every time. Some people, especially those who by temperament are Free-and-Fearless, seldom do things out of habit. Making a habit of brushing their teeth may even be a problem for them! Not many of their choices are "what they always do."

Other temperament types may not always make E choices that way either. A People Person may switch to a different brand of shampoo if a best friend is along on a shopping trip and pushes a new brand. A Sane-and-Sensible may change to a brand suggested by a consumer report, and a Considering-and-Careful may decide to run an experiment on shampoos, trying several different ones before deciding which they like best.

For many E choices, however, doing things out of habit, the way we've always done them, moves most people along without lots of thought and hassles.

I think my grandma makes a lot of her choices out of habit. For example, when I visit her and ask what we're going to do that day, she always says, "Let's go to the movies."

Maybe she is a Sane-and-Sensible. People of that type like to choose what they know best. There's nothing wrong with that if you like your choice and it works well for you.

Choosing the same old things, however, can make you miss a lot of neat things in life. For example, if you always watch a sitcom on TV and won't try watching a travelogue, you may miss finding out about a place you'd like to visit. If you always pass up the egg roll to take the spaghetti in the school cafeteria, you may miss trying something that tastes great.

Not my sister! She eats something weird every time my parents take us out for dinner. She'll order something just because she says it "looks good" on the menu.

When she makes a quick choice like that she is using the third way to choose. We call it "catch the moment." For many easy and some middle-sized choices, catching the moment works much of the time. You look at a situation, size it up quickly, and make a choice. Free-and-Fearless types prefer this method for E, M, and even H choices—not always a smart choice on their part.

But catching the moment is used by all types some of the time because it can add excitement to life and lead to some fun times. What would you do if your mom said, "Everyone in the car—let's go to that ball game you've all been talking about. My boss gave me tickets"?

Wow, I'd be in the car in a flash! I like that part of catching the moment. Am I catching the moment if I decide to sit with a new kid in the cafeteria, even if I almost always sit at another table?

Right. You are catching the moment rather than choosing what you usually choose or choosing what you think someone else wants. You don't give your choice of table a lot of thought; catching the moment is no big deal.

Catching the moment as a way of making middle-sized choices, however, is often not a great idea. Most of the time, you need to say "Mmm…" and survey the situation before choosing. For example, if you catch the moment by suddenly inviting lots of friends to your house after a big soccer game without warning your parents, you might not be making the wisest choice.

If a dozen hungry, thirsty kids suddenly walked into our house, I'd catch a lot more than the moment!
Unless you have parents who understand that teenagers of any type are pretty likely to make a lot of fun choices by catching the moment.

Not my parents! We were walking past a shoe store the other day and I wanted to catch the moment—go in the store and buy a great looking pair that I saw in the window and have been wanting for some time. My dad said the shoes were superexpensive and then he said no loud and clear. Mom said my wanting them was just a whim and I'd get tired of them fast.
Your mom was telling you that catching the moment is not the right way to make a choice about shoes that cost a lot of money.

But I really wasn't catching the moment in making the choice. I was just catching the moment about the time to buy them. I had thought *a lot* about getting them. How can I get my parents to change their minds?

What have you said or done since then to convince your parents that buying those shoes is a good choice?

Well, I've told them all my friends have a pair. I even sat on my bed one afternoon and wouldn't eat dinner.

Begging and whining and sulking are little kid tricks. Sometimes you will get what you want by begging and whining, but only because you wear your parents down. When parents see childish behaviors like that, they feel they can't trust you to make an intelligent choice.

But if you can show them how you made your choice and why you think it is a good one, they may let you make choices not only about your shoes, but also about other things because they see you behaving more like a young person who can be trusted to make a good decision.

Are you saying you'll guarantee that if I say the right words I can get whatever I want?

No, no, not that! Your parents may have a good reason for saying no. We are simply saying that you send adults a message by the way you choose and the way you explain how and why you made your choice. The message is either that you made a careful, thoughtful choice or that you didn't.

Your parents want some solid reasons for spending a good bit of your family's money. You have only told them you want the shoes because your friends have them. That kind of reason is what made your mom say you'll get tired of them. She thinks you are being influenced by your friends to choose what they want and you won't want the shoes once you have them.

Then how do I give them the message that what I want would be a good choice? I really do have some good reasons.

Then read on and we'll tell you how to "picture the possibilities." You need to picture the possibilities of your choices not only for yourself so you can make a good choice, but also for your parents, so they can understand why you think buying the shoes is a good choice for you.

▶ *Take a few moments now to consider the way you went about making some recent choices by filling in the chart on the following page. Write down the choices you made, then rate them according to what kind of choices they were—E for easy, M for middle-sized, or H for hard. Then we'll talk about how you can make better choices by picturing the possibilities.*

Choices You Made Recently

When you chose what you thought others wanted you to choose:

Was it an E, M, or H choice? ❑ E ❑ M ❑ H

When you chose what you've always chosen:

Was it an E, M, or H choice? ❑ E ❑ M ❑ H

When you caught the moment:

Was it an E, M, or H choice? ❑ E ❑ M ❑ H

4

Picturing the Possibilities

You:	Wow! Look at those horses. They're beautiful. Can I take a picture?
Your brother:	Hey, no fair! Dad! Didn't you say I could take the next picture?
Camera:	Click!
Dad:	The way you two were grabbing and shooting that camera without aiming, I doubt if the picture will be any good at all.

Before you try to persuade your parents to do something like buying the expensive shoes you want, you should think about how to "picture the possibilities." It combines aspects of all four temperaments and helps you take into account both facts and feelings.

Is that how I can persuade my parents to let me get my shoes?

Picturing the possibilities for yourself helps you to be sure that you still think buying them is a good choice. If you do, then you can picture the possibilities for your parents.

Let's compare making a choice to taking a photograph. You catch the moment if you point a camera and snap a picture of whatever is in front of the lens. It may be a good shot or it may not. When you picture the possibilities, you take the time to frame your shot and think about how the finished picture will look. By doing so, you have a much better chance of getting a good photo.

Just as you may or may not take a good picture if you catch the moment, you may or may not make a good choice if you catch the moment. If you picture the possibilities, you increase the chances that you will make the right choice and that you can get someone else to agree with you that it is a good choice.

Picturing the possibilities sounds like a hard thing to do.

Picturing the possibilities is a lot easier for some people than for others because it is a four-step process. If by temperament you tend to be one of those give-me-action, Free-and-Fearless types or a concerned-about-others People Person type, this process may feel like a waste of time. No matter what your type, however, picturing the possibilities isn't hard once you get the hang of it, and it is absolutely necessary for survival in the adult world.

Why is it so useful?

First, picturing the possibilities gives you a clear look at your choices and what will probably happen to you if you make a certain choice—key to making an important H choice and helpful, too, for M and even some E choices.

Second, if you follow the four steps carefully, you'll know why you've made the choice you have. That makes you feel good about your choice. Moreover, you always have a super explanation when you want someone else to accept your choice, especially if other people (like adults!) don't agree with your decision. Making a good case for your choice never hurts.

So what are the four steps? This sounds like something I can use.

To picture the possibilities, follow these four steps:

1. Know what your choices are.

2. Find the facts that will help you know more about those choices.

3. Look at the possible outcomes for each of the choices.

4. Ask yourself if your choice feels right.

I thought maybe picture the possibilities means to actually draw a picture.

That's not a bad idea, if you like to draw. Let's take an example and see how the four-step process works. Suppose you are trying to decide whether to go to a school party or take a baby-sitting job on Friday night.

In this case, you have three choices: You can stay home, go to the party, or baby-sit. You've already ruled out staying home, so we'll toss out that choice as not being one to consider.

On the top half of your paper, draw a picture of you at the party. On the bottom half, draw a picture of you baby-sitting. If you don't like to draw, just write down your two choices.

I think I'll just write down the two choices. Now what should I do?

Under each, write why you think it would be a good choice under the heading "Pro" and why you think it would be a bad choice under the heading "Con"—as we did.

Baby-sit

Pro	Con
Earn money.	Miss out on some fun.
Have time to finish a book report when kids are asleep.	Have to explain to my friends why I'm not going.
Help our neighbors.	

Next, think about what pros and cons you would give a friend who was trying to make the same choice.

Asking your parents and your friends if there are some other pros and cons you haven't thought of is also a good idea.

Why ask them? Isn't this my choice?

It is your choice, but your parents and friends may give you extra ideas and information that you don't know about or haven't considered. In deciding how to spend Friday night, maybe you didn't know that your cousin is coming to town and that he might come over to help you baby-sit. Add that to the pro or con side (depending on what you think of your cousin!).

The more pros and cons you are able to list, the better view you'll have of your choices and the more information you'll have if you need to explain your choice to other people.

Listing those things takes lots of time.

It can take some time. But if the choice is a hard one to make, this step is important. Taking the time to consider any choice helps you make a good one, but if you are a Considering-and-Careful or People Person type, you probably tend to rely on your feelings more than facts. People of these types must make a special effort to get all the available facts.

Okay, after I list everything, then what?

When you have written down everything you can think of, go over the list to see which choice has the most pros and the fewest cons.

Then that's my final choice?

Not quite. Now think about the outcomes of each choice. Ask yourself how you will be affected by each choice if you make it.

I guess if I choose to baby-sit, I'll have money to put toward a CD and have more free time the rest of the weekend. If I go to the party, I'll have fun and won't feel left out of the talk Monday at school.

Those are the short-term outcomes to consider, and, since baby-sitting is an M choice, you don't have to worry about long-term outcomes.

With H choices, however, the long-term outcomes may be the most important piece of picturing the possibilities. You have to ask yourself, "How will this choice affect my life in the months or years ahead?"

For example, suppose you are choosing the kind of bike helmet to buy. You know that of the two you would consider buying, one is much cheaper than the other and if you bought it you would have money left over for other things you want to buy. But when you look at the facts, you see that the more expensive one would protect your head much better in the event of a fall. Comparing possible long-term outcomes helps you to squeeze your allowance hard and choose the better helmet. The head you save will be your own.

Take a look at the chart labeled "When You Have Choices to Make" on the next page. We filled the chart in using the bike helmet example we just discussed. Considering your options this carefully can help you picture the possible outcomes of your choices and make choices that are right for you. In this case, buying the more expensive helmet was the optimal choice.

▶ *Take a few moments now to look over the chart on the following page. Then, try this technique to work through a choice you're currently facing by turning to the next page and filling out that chart using the bike helmet chart as a model. It can help you to think through and picture the possibilities of your own choices. When you're done, we'll talk some more about picturing the possibilities.*

When You Have Choices to Make

Choice #1
Buy cheap helmet.

Pros	**Cons**
Money left for tapes	Crack easier
Like color better	Thinner shell
Friends have this one —	
it's ok	

Outcome?
May get hurt.

Choice #2
Buy expensive helmet.

Pros	**Cons**
Safer if I fall	Take all my savings
Outer shell thicker	Awful color
Biker's group	
recommends	

Outcome?
Protect my head better.

Decision: #1_____ or #2 ✔_____ Does this choice feel right? Yes ✔___ No____
If not, what other choices, or combination of choices, do you have?

When You Have Choices to Make

Choice #1

Pros	Cons
_____	_____
_____	_____
_____	_____
_____	_____

Outcome?

....

Choice #1

Pros	Cons
_____	_____
_____	_____
_____	_____
_____	_____

Outcome?

....

Decision: #1____ or #2____ Does this choice feel right? Yes____ No____
If not, what other choices, or combination of choices, do you have?

After I think about the outcomes, do I make my final choice?

Yes. But once you have decided which choice to make, ask yourself if it feels right in the pit of your stomach. If your choice makes you feel uneasy, you probably didn't find all the pros and cons. For instance, if you decide to go to the party Friday night instead of baby-sitting, and your choice just doesn't feel right, you should reconsider your choice.

This is the time when the Free-and-Fearless and Sane-and-Sensible types, who tend to rely on facts more than on their feelings, should reach deep inside themselves and listen to what their feelings are telling them.

I can see that picturing the possibilities is important for M and H choices, but you said it is sometimes important for E choices. I don't see why spending time to picture the possibilities matters if I'm making an easy choice.

Sometimes those small E choices can add up. Suppose you ignore someone when you are near them because you don't like that person. The way you choose to act will soon send a clear message about your opinion of him or her not only to the person but also to others who are around both of you. Picturing the possibilities of E actions that fall into a pattern or become a habit is important.

For example, we said that deciding what to wear is an E choice and not a big deal. For any given day, it isn't. But what if someone *always* chooses to wear the kind of clothes worn by people who belong to a particular group? Pretty soon, you begin to think that person belongs to the group, whether they do or not. And if that group happened to be a gang, it would mean big trouble.

I think I know what you mean. One girl at school used to get along okay with everyone. This year she started acting as if she's bored with her classes and just putting up with everyone and everything. At first we thought she was having a few bad days, but now we think she's got an attitude.

People develop an attitude by not paying enough attention to E choices. No single E choice makes much of a difference, but when there's a pattern to E choices in the way you walk, talk, hold your head, wear your clothes, or look at others, people begin to see these behaviors as the real you.

So if your choice is an important H or M one, or even an E one that could grow in importance, picturing the possibilities helps you to see your options.

Hmm-mm. Well, I guess I do need to put some more thought into choosing those shoes.

You might even change your own mind. You might decide you'd rather ask for money to spend on a new jacket.

If you still feel that buying the shoes is a good choice, show your parents how you came to that decision. Put your reasons in writing. They will be pretty impressed that you have thought through the issues. They might even change their minds.

That doesn't mean that they will always see things your way. They may have thought about some more pros and cons that they haven't mentioned. If they tell you no, then go along with their choice as pleasantly as you can.

That doesn't seem fair.

Well, there's an old saying and it's true, even though none of us likes to hear it—"Life isn't fair." But there's more than fairness involved in not making a scene when your parents don't agree with you. Parents can sometimes picture possibilities that you can't.

I'm not sure what you mean.

Suppose you try to tell your five-year-old neighbor that you have a big test tomorrow and that you need to study your math instead of playing with her. Because she hasn't yet had the experience of taking a math test, she can't possibly picture the possibilities the way you can. She can't imagine the time it takes to go over formulas and practice problems.

Are you saying that I can't always picture the possibilities the way my parents do because I haven't had the experiences they've had?

On the nose! Because of their experiences, good and bad, your parents may make choices—like refusing to get you the shoes—that don't make sense to you or don't even seem right for you. But, because they care for you, they try to make the best choices they can.

Well, my neighbor says they'll start needing me to baby-sit a lot more. Then I can buy whatever I want. I'll have lots of my own money.

Then you'll really need to know how to make choices. With more money in your pocket, you'll be tempted to make quick choices, and quick picks are even harder to make, as you'll soon see.

▶ *Now, before reading on, take a few minutes to do some exercises that will give you some practice in making choices. You can think over the following scenarios yourself, or talk about them with your classmates, friends, or parents. Try to put yourself in the place of the person who's making the choice in the story and choose the decision that you think would be best for that person. After you've made all your choices, share them with others.*

Lunch Time Study Session

The food line in the school cafeteria stretched all the way to the door. Carlin sighed, took his place at the end, pulled his test notes from his pocket and read, for the umpteenth time, the names of the thirteen original colonies. By the time he reached the food counter, he had them pretty well memorized, all but the Carolinas. He kept forgetting them. *New Hampshire, Massachusetts, Connecticut*...he repeated to himself. Out loud, he said, "Pizza, please." *Rhode Island, New York, New Jersey....* "Yes, please, salad, too." *Pennsylvania, Delaware, Maryland, Virginia....*

He reached for an oatmeal cookie while he tried to remember what came next. *"The Carolinas!"* he suddenly said out loud in triumph and whirled around with his tray—right into the tray of short-but-sweet Mercedes, knocking her chocolate pudding right down the back of Rodger, the school's meanest football player.

Carlin's Choices: What Should He Do?

(a) Point to Mercedes and say that she did it, even if it meant losing her friendship.

(b) Drop his tray and run. It might be worth getting detention for running in the cafeteria just to get away from Rodger before he could see who did it.

(c) Punch Rodger before he could punch him and hope Rodger would be too shocked to fight back.

(d) Say to Rodger, "Gee, man, I'm clumsy. Let me go to the gym and get you a clean T-shirt. Sorry about that."

(e) Yell for the cafeteria monitor to come over before Rodger can say or do anything.

(f) Offer to get a mop and clean up the mess.

(g) Throw his salad on Mercedes and yell, "Food fight!", hoping that Rodger would think the chocolate pudding was just part of the fun.

(h) What other choices could Carlin make?

President Serina

Serina lay on her bed and thought about the student council race. She could just see herself as president, holding the little gavel and shutting up people like that gabby Linda when she tried to make everyone do things her way. *It'll be a cinch for me to win. I've been class representative every year,* Serina thought to herself. *When I'm president, I'll get those water fountains in the gym fixed and I'll start some more school clubs, too....* Just then, the phone rang. It had to be Chen, her best friend. She always knew when to call.

"Serina, guess what!" said Chen. "I've decided to run for student council president. My dad says he'll buy me my own computer if I win. I want you to be my campaign manager. Deal?"

Serina's Choices: What Should She Do?

(a) Tell Chen she's on her own. Run for council president against Chen and hope she will still be friends if she loses.

(b) Consider friendship first and help Chen, even though she, Serina, had always planned to be president.

(c) Tell Chen that it's no deal, but she'd like Chen to help run her campaign instead.

(d) Suggest that the two of them forget it. Being president would take a lot of time after school when they could be having fun hanging out at the rec center.

(e) Join forces with Linda and beat that double-dealing Chen. After all, Chen knew Serina always planned to be president.

(f) What other choices could Serina make?

I've Changed My Mind

Tyronne put down his money and signed up for two weeks of football camp the first day they let him register. "Football is your future," his dad told him. And this year the camp would be coached by a former Baltimore Colt quarterback! Not just some high school coach—the real thing! Since the coach was one of his dad's heroes, Tyronne's father was also thrilled about the chance to meet the ex-pro on Parents' Day at the camp.

Every day Tyronne counted down the days to June 25. Until this letter came from his Uncle Jarrel:

> Dear Tyronne,
> I bet you thought I was joking last summer. Well, I wasn't. I am really going to sail as a deckhand on a yacht to the Caribbean this summer, and there is an opening for a cabin boy. I have already put your name in. The job pays well and it's yours if you want it. We sail June 30.
> See you then!
> —Uncle Jarrel

Tyronne's Choices: What Should He Do?

(a) Go with his uncle—he'd never have another chance like that—and hope that he'd make the team even if he didn't go to football camp.

(b) Ask his uncle if he can sail later in the summer.

(c) Go to opening day of the football camp and explain to the coach why he wouldn't finish, even though it would mean that some other kid wouldn't be able to go to the camp in his place.

(d) Go to as many days of the football camp as he could. Then pretend to get hurt so he could get away without having to tell the coach about the Caribbean trip.

(e) Go to football camp.

(f) What other choices could Tyronne make?

5

Picking a Quick Plan or Planning a Quick Pick

Mom:	We're here at the beach to enjoy our vacation. We don't want any accidents, so don't go out into the deep water.
You:	Don't worry, Mom, I'll be okay.
Mom:	And if the lifeguard blows her whistle, pay attention.
You:	Mom, I know, I know.
Mom:	And if you decide to walk down the boardwalk, tell me. And, remember....

Picturing the possibilities takes some thought on your part, and that kind of thinking takes time, especially when the process is new to you. However, just as stores stack lots of great things at a checkout counter to lure you into parting with your money on the spot, you will also face lots of situations that lure you into making a quick pick that may not be your best choice.

**Sometimes when I have to decide in a hurry, I feel
trapped into going along with something when I know**

what I'm doing isn't really right. Figuring out what to say and do then is really tough.

It isn't easy at all. As adults, we sometimes act as if making the right decision should be easy for you when you're asked to do something wrong by your friends, or by people you want to be your friends, or maybe even by people who scare you. In truth, however, standing up and doing something different from the rest of the crowd is one of the hardest choices a teen can make.

To be sure that you will make the right choice at times when you are under pressure, you should try to decide *before* you are confronted with a difficult situation what choice you will make. That way, if you are suddenly put on the spot, you'll know what your choice is and you can say it in a tone of voice that makes others realize that you mean it. Deciding in advance may not be something your temperament type usually does; if so, situations like these are a good time to go against your type.

So what should I say if I'm in a situation like that?

Only you can make that choice, but don't wait until you are in the situation and find yourself feeling trapped. One afternoon soon, hide out in your favorite place where you can think and not be bothered. Make a list of serious choices you might face in the next year or two. Start with the problems we list here and add some of your own. Think how you want to handle each situation if someone pressures you. Think what you would say in a difficult situation if you:

- Like the person

- Want the person to like you

- Feel threatened by the person

Practice saying aloud the answers you decide are best for you for the situations listed and for others that you think of. When you run into these kinds of problems, you'll find that sticking to your choice is a lot easier if you already know what your choice is and how you are going to explain it to others.

> ▶ *Take a few moments now to think about and respond to the situations presented in the exercise on the following pages. Also, add any other situations that you can think of. When you're done, we'll talk more about picturing the possibilities of choices.*

Picturing the possibilities before situations occur can help you to be clear in your mind what your personal choices would be and why. Planning ahead will also help you feel more sure of yourself if you need to stick with your choice when you are confronted by others. And planning ahead and thinking about situations that might occur can even help you avoid trouble and danger.

My parents are always telling me to watch out for this, be sure to do that, be careful of something else. Always thinking about the worst thing that can happen takes the fun out of everything.

Parents, no matter what their type, worry about their kids. And it's a good thing, too. For example, if you listen to your parents, you will think ahead and not ride your bike on a road where the traffic is terrible. Or, before you go boating alone, you will let someone know when and where you are going and you will wear a life jacket the whole time in case the boat should tip.

What Would You Say?

Situation: "Why don't we egg the principal's house?"

If You Like the Person _____

_____

If You Want the Person to Like You _____

_____

If You Feel Threatened by the Person _____

_____

Situation: "Help me cheat on this test."

If You Like the Person _____

_____

If You Want the Person to Like You _____

_____

If You Feel Threatened by the Person _____

_____

Situation: "C'mon. Take a drink!"

If You Like the Person _____

_____

If You Want the Person to Like You _____

_____

If You Feel Threatened by the Person _____

_____

Situation: *"Want to smoke?"*

If You Like the Person _____

_____

If You Want the Person to Like You _____

_____

If You Feel Threatened by the Person _____

_____

Situation: *"Hey, let's skip school today."*

If You Like the Person _____

_____

If You Want the Person to Like You _____

_____

If You Feel Threatened by the Person _____

_____

Situation: *"I dare you to steal those baseball cards."*

If You Like the Person _____

_____

If You Want the Person to Like You _____

_____

If You Feel Threatened by the Person _____

_____

But planning ahead doesn't have to spoil your fun. Learning to do basic planning on your own without waiting for someone to remind you is one more sign that you are growing up. The more adventuresome your plans, the more important it is for you to think ahead. Follow the example of race car drivers who plan for every eventuality before they ever set foot in their cars. This allows them to be prepared when the unexpected occurs.

We know that the very idea of planning for the worst does not come easily for some types, especially the Free-and-Fearless type, who prefers not to plan ahead, or the People Person type, who prefers to think that only good things will happen. But in some situations, we all need to be more like the Sane-and-Sensible person, who considers the possibility that the worst *can* happen and prepares in advance to deal with it, or like the Considering-and-Careful person, who enjoys long-range planning. We don't have to dwell on negative possibilities, just be prepared for them should they occur.

I remember when I was in third grade, our class went to visit the fire department. The firefighter said we should talk with our parents about what we should do if we woke up and smelled smoke. When I told my dad that I was scared our house would catch on fire, he hung an escape ladder outside my bedroom window. Is that the sort of thing you mean?

That's a good example of planning. Your dad didn't want you to be unprotected if the house caught on fire, and he knew that if you had an escape ladder you wouldn't need to worry about it.

In the example you mentioned, your dad did the planning for you, but for most situations that you will be faced with now, *you* will need to be the one to take charge. For example, are you ever home alone?

Sometimes. I usually get home from school an hour or so before my parents come home from work.

Then you definitely need to think ahead and be prepared in case some problem arises.

Our house has never caught on fire.

We're glad to hear it! But we aren't talking just about emergencies like the house catching on fire. We're also talking about being prepared to make a quick and good choice when you are faced with everyday problems that are as simple as forgetting your house key on a rainy day or coping with no electricity if the power suddenly goes off. To be better prepared for making quick M and E choices as well as H ones, ask a parent to think through with you the problems that might arise when you are home alone. Decide together what you should do if any of these things happen. How would you respond, for example, if someone knocked at the door while you were home alone?

▶ *Take a few moments now to think through this kind of situation by doing the exercise on the following page. Use the steps listed to think through the situation so you can be prepared. Then, we'll talk some more about preparing for the unexpected.*

Choices to Make When You're Home Alone and a Visitor Knocks

Place a check mark in the box next to the choices that you are comfortable with. Cross out the choices that do not seem to be good ones for you.

❑ **1** Look through window or peephole.

❑ **2** Call neighbor or parent so someone is on phone while you open door.

❑ **3** Ignore the knocking and keep on with what you are doing.

❑ **4** Quietly go in back room and hide behind door.

❑ **5** _____

Now, think about what facts can help you make the best choice from the choices that you've checked off.

	Pros	Cons
Choice #1	_____	_____
	_____	_____

Possible Outcome

	Pros	Cons
Choice # 2	_____	_____
	_____	_____

Possible Outcome

	Pros	Cons
Choice # 3	_____	_____
	_____	_____

Possible Outcome

Final Choice: Choice #_____. Does this choice feel right? Yes____ No____
If not, what other choices, or combination of choices, do you have?

But what if I'm caught off guard by something I can't possibly have imagined?

Even though planning ahead helps when you have to handle many difficult choices in life, you are bound to be faced with the unexpected. In a crisis situation, the outcome of events depends only about 10 percent on what happens, but about 90 percent on how you handle it. That means how you react to a situation more strongly influences the outcome than the event itself.

Imagine that you are riding your bike, for example. Because it is a warm, sunny day, you are wearing shorts. Suddenly, a huge barking dog shoots out from behind a tree and menaces you, biting at your leg with teeth that you'll see in your dreams for years to come. What will you do?

Wow! I don't know. I sure wouldn't have time to make a chart that pictures the possibilities. I guess if I see someone running to help me, I could stop riding and put my leg up on the handlebars. Hmm. I'd have to think about other choices....

Right. In this kind of situation, you need to use your head!—to picture the possibilities, that is. Simply catching the moment and responding in panic seldom works in a **super H** situation. A super H situation is an unexpected one in which:

- You may be seriously hurt

- You know that whatever choice you make involves some risk and danger

- You need to choose what to do in a hurry

So what can I do in a super H situation?

We can't possibly give you steps that will cover every super H situation you may be confronted with during your life. We hope they will be few. But when you are in a super bad spot in which you must make a quick choice, keep these general guidelines in mind:

- **Don't panic.** Easier said than done, we know. But giving in to a feeling that you are powerless and can't do anything is equal to giving up. Don't curse or scream or run, simply to feel you are doing something. That's just plain foolish. Instead, take one or two deep breaths to help you relax if you have even a moment or two to think.

- **Protect yourself physically if you can while you try to think of a good option.** If you are hurt in some way, thinking straight about good choices will be harder.

- **Do what you can to buy or gain time.** Time is often on your side; act in a way that will protect you physically and give you some time to think clearly. Depending on the situation, that time could be anywhere from a split second to much longer.

- **Picture the possibilities in your mind.** In the time you have, consider your choices, the pros and cons, and the possible outcomes.

- **Carefully choose when to take a risk.** Risk taking involves making a deliberate choice to actively try to get yourself out of your predicament at the best possible moment.

I guess Free-and-Fearless types are more likely to take risks without thinking the situation through.

Yes, they are. They are often good in emergencies because they seem to have a sixth sense about the outcome of a risk; however, people of any type can, as the old saying goes, "rise to the occasion." You are always smarter and stronger in an emergency than you think.

> ▶ *Take a few moments now to look at the exercise on the following page and think about and prepare for an unexpected crisis—one that can occur while you're baby-sitting. After picking a situation, use the steps listed in the exercise to consider your choices and reach a decision about how you should handle the problem. When you're done, we'll talk some more about making quick decisions.*

Thank goodness I haven't had to face many emergencies like that dog. In fact, most of the times I have to make really quick choices I'm just put on the spot by a friend. If friends say everyone is going to the mall to see a TV star and Mom's told me that she wants me to help her at home this afternoon, I never know what to say.

In that kind of situation, since your life is not in danger, you do not need to go through all the steps you would in a super H situation. You do need to stop for a minute to mentally picture the possibilities. List the pros and cons and the outcomes in your head. Picture yourself meeting the star. Picture getting a photo taken of yourself standing next to the star. Picture your mom's face if you don't show up and picture what she'll do. Picture yourself grounded for a month. Check out which choice makes your insides feel better.

Choices to Make When You're Baby-sitting and Something Goes Wrong

What's gone wrong?_____

You could choose to

1.

or

2.

or

3.

What are the pros and cons of your choices?

Pros	*Cons*
_____	_____
_____	_____

Pros	*Cons*
_____	_____
_____	_____

Pros	*Cons*
_____	_____
_____	_____

You choose to

Picture the outcome of your top choice

....

....

Does this choice feel right? Yes_____ No_____ If not, rethink your choice. Ask someone to read what you wrote. How does this person feel about your decision? What other information might you consider?

On that one, I'd choose to go home. No TV star is worth being grounded for a month. Do I tell my friends, "My insides tell me to go home"? They'd really think I'd flipped.

No, there's no need for that. All you need to say is, "Thanks, but I can't go this time." You don't have to explain. You don't owe them an explanation or an apology. They should accept your decision. If your friends pester you or ask you for an explanation, simply say, "My mom will ground me 'till I'm 50 years old if I don't go home." Then move away.

If friends tease you or threaten not to be friends or get mean, keep your cool and keep moving. Arguing will get you confused and stressed. Fighting will only add to your troubles. A true friend may not like your choice but will not stay mad. If someone stays mad, then you don't need that kind of person for a friend.

Most of the time my friends have great ideas that I can go along with. Like last week, someone suggested that we enter our dogs in a county dog show. I wanted to say a quick yes. You know, catch the moment! But my dog gets real upset in a crowd, jumps around and barks like crazy, so I decided to just go to the show with the other kids and leave Terry the Terror Terrier at home. I know my friends don't like my dog as much as I do.

Sounds as if you made a great choice by mentally picturing the outcome and deciding a show for your dog didn't feel right. You made a choice that was good for you and your pup. It was also good for your friends. Very often you'll find, as in this case, that a choice you make doesn't just affect you, but can affect others, too. So let's talk about what that has to do with how you choose.

6

Choosing Sometimes Means Losing

You: Wow! I can't believe our luck. The only store in town that still has this T-shirt everyone's wearing. And it's on sale. (To clerk) I'd like one of these in a large size.

Friend: Same for me.

Clerk: I'm sorry, we have only one large left. Would you like to see some other shirts we have that are similar?

Many times, when you choose, you aren't the only one affected. Your choices can be pretty important to other people, too.

For instance, suppose your brother is expecting a call and asks you to stay off the phone. If you and your friend tie up the phone for a long time, consider how that choice affects your brother.

Come on! Staying on the phone is a pretty small deal.

True, but small choices that take into account the special feelings of others can help family life go more smoothly.

Are you saying I should stay off the phone? No way!

How about making another choice? Talk a few minutes and tell your friend you'll call back later. You use the phone but you *compromise* with your brother by not staying on very long.

When you compromise, you give up a little of what you would most like and the other person does the same. That way, you both feel good about your choice. Compromising often works to smooth out situations because both people win and feel good about the outcome. Whenever your choice affects others, a choice that makes everyone feel like a winner is a good one.

With most of my choices, I don't think anyone else is involved.

More often than you may think, other people are. You are at an age where everyone is likely to do what the first kid does. No one wants to look different or chicken. So if you take the first can of beer at a party, you may influence someone else to take a drink. Likewise, if you are the first person in your class to volunteer to help some younger schoolchildren with reading, others may follow your lead.

If you choose to go out for a sport and you get a spot on the team, you essentially knock someone else off the team. If you choose to go steady with someone, that person is no longer free to go out with others. If you choose to recycle bottles and cans, you help save natural resources for the benefit of everyone. You *are* a crucial link in the chain of life whether you want to be or not.

I guess I'm pretty important after all.

You bet you are, and don't ever forget it.

But choosing works two ways. What if choices other people make cause me lots of grief? My best friend's parents are getting divorced. The kids will be split up between them—the girls going with the mom and the boys going with the dad.

You're right. Other people's choices can affect you, too. Sometimes the choices adults make can hurt kids a lot. Deciding to split up forced your friend's parents to make some hard choices. They certainly didn't mean to hurt you. They were only trying to do what they thought was best for their family.

They may think they made the best choice, but they're messing up my life. I may never see my best friend again. I wish I could do something to keep my friend from moving away.

Not being able to take charge and do something can give you a feeling of teeth-grinding frustration. We certainly want to help you take control of your life, or we wouldn't have written this book!

But we're here to tell you that, regardless of age, *you can only control and be responsible for yourself and your own choices.*

Well, their choice sure hurts all the same!

The best thing you can do is to accept their decision, since there is nothing you can do about it. It's not within your control. Then look for some way to help *you* make good choices that will move you past the bad times. For instance, you could consider doing the following:

- Try reading stories of famous people who found ways to live through the bad things that happened in their lives when they were young. A librarian can help you find such books.

- Find a new friend, a new sport, or a new hobby. Getting involved in something new will help take your mind off how much you hurt.

- Talk with your parents or another adult, such as your favorite teacher or a guidance counselor, about how you feel. Somewhere there are adults who care about you and will help you get over the rough situation you find yourself in.

Making choices can be really complicated, can't it?

Truly. When choices affect other people, those affected in turn often make choices that affect still others—often including the original choice maker. So, for example, the choice your friend's parents are making to split their family affects you. Although you cannot change or control that choice, you will make choices of your own as a result of theirs.

Let's say your friend moves to another town. Every week your old friend calls you on the phone to talk. For the first month, you are glad to talk, but soon you are more interested in a new friend you have chosen. Your old friend becomes hurt and no longer wants you to come spend the summer together the way you two planned before you separated.

The point is this: Based on what you do, other people make choices. Their choices can then circle back to affect *you* and start the cycle all over again.

Even when you try to picture the possibilities, choosing can become confusing and complicated when the cycles of choice making broaden to include more choices and actions on the part of others. The final consequences can sometimes be hard for anyone to have pictured.

I saw that happen just recently. A girl in my math group took a toy gun to class for fun. At lunch, we all laughed and pretended to shoot back at her. But when the principal saw the gun, she called the girl's parents, the police, and all kinds of people because there is a school rule about guns—toy or real. The girl ended up being suspended, and then she was sent to another school. She never dreamed something like that would happen.

That's a great example of someone making a choice that set in motion the choices of others, ending with a final result that had an impact on lots of people—like you—to whom the whole incident at first seemed rather small and meaningless.

Don't you think she got an H punishment for making an E choice?

Whenever you break a rule at school, no matter how unimportant it seems to you, you run the risk of school authorities seeing your behavior as an M or even an H choice, even if in your mind it is only an E. "No big deal" does not seem to be part of the language principals use! The girl may have thought that breaking the rule about having a toy gun at school was no big deal, but guns are getting to be such a problem in many schools that no teacher or principal treats them lightly anymore.

Our principal said that the reason the girl got in so much trouble was because she broke a state law. I can't believe there's a state law about toy guns.

Hard as it may be for you to believe, there are laws that cover all kinds of behaviors—even, in some places, carrying toy guns. And anytime you break a law, you are making a real H choice, even though you may not know it at the time.

If I start thinking too hard about how important it is for me to make the right choices and how I might affect others, things get cloudy and I'm not sure what I should do. I sometimes think I'm better off *not* picturing the possibilities.

You're right that making a choice can start to seem more and more complex as you add more information to help you make your decision. But that's the point: Very few H and M type choices are simple.

However, if you find yourself feeling overwhelmed by facts and feelings and confused by the events that you might set in motion, stop thinking about your choices for a while. Most anyone can become confused by planning if you think *too* hard about something. If it happens to you, take a time-out. Go to a movie or the mall, talk about fun stuff with friends, play a game, take a walk, sleep on your problem for a night—anything to take your mind off the choices facing you. When you return to your problem, things might very well be clearer. At the least, you'll be making a choice when you are fresh.

I try to make good choices. I really do. But what if I make a really dumb choice? And what should I do if I change my mind about a choice I've made?

Those are things we all do sometimes. You raise some good questions. Let's talk about how to handle those kinds of problems.

▶ *Now take a few moments to look at two situations. These situations will give you some practice in making difficult choices that require some consideration of how choices can affect others. Try to put yourself in the place of the person involved in the situation, and make the choice you feel is best for them. Keep in mind how the choice will impact others. In both cases, any choice the person makes will stir up some complex reactions from others involved.*

Branching Out

Hannah loved playing the clarinet. She spent hours practicing every day. One evening her mother told her how worried she was that Hannah was spending too much time alone, lost in her music. "I've talked to your teacher and she agrees that you need to be out more, having new experiences, trying new things, and being with your friends and family."

Things to Consider

- What should Hannah consider doing?

- What choices can she make?

- What compromise solutions can she suggest to her mom?

Can I Take a Raincheck?

John knew how much next weekend's camping trip with his Aunt Barbara and her family meant to everyone. His mom was pleased that the entire family would be together for this long-planned outing. And Aunt Barbara was his favorite relative, although he considered Aunt Barbara's son Matt, who was two years younger than John, a pain. But Matt idolized him and followed him around whenever they were together. As Aunt Barbara said, "You can help him learn a lot about the outdoors. I'm counting on you, John." John enjoyed camping and figured he'd have a pretty good time. Teaching Matt what he knew about camping and the woods might even be fun.

Then his friend Gary called. "Hey, my family is taking a ski trip up in the mountains next weekend. We even have a great log cabin and all the equipment we need is already rented. Dad said I can invite one friend, so I picked you. You've always said you wanted to learn to ski, and my dad's a great teacher."

Things to Consider

- What do you think John should choose to do?

- How do you think the other people affected by his choice will feel—his mom? Aunt Barbara? Matt? Gary?

7

Changing Your Plans

You: Mom, I'm going to the mall with Chris.

Mom: Oh, dear, I forgot to tell you that Pat called
about your both going biking this afternoon.

You: Wow! I'd rather do that! Now what do I tell Chris?
I may hurt Chris' feelings if I tell the truth. But I
hate to miss a chance for some fun biking. I wonder
if Chris will find out if I make up an excuse for not
going to the mall.... Hmm-mm—What to do?

No matter how you choose and whether the choice is an E, M, or H one,
you will sometimes change your mind about a choice you made and
want to make a different one.

**But sometimes changing your mind isn't all that easy.
Last week I agreed with some friends to wear a certain
kind of sweatshirt to school one day, but then I decided I
didn't want to. When I showed up in a different one, my
friends were mad and wanted to know why I changed my
mind. What should I have said?**

Most times, if you change your mind about an E choice, as this one was, no reason is needed. With good friends, all you need to say is, "I changed my mind." If they push you, add "That's the way I am sometimes," and then ask one of them about something else, like whether they studied for today's math test.

One friend got really mad, a lot more than I had figured on. I mean, what's a sweatshirt?

Talk to your friend. Try to find out if your friend was really angry about your choice not to wear the sweatshirt or felt personally rejected by you. You would not use those words, for sure, but you'd say you want to know if he or she was upset about the shirt itself or perhaps felt you weren't a good friend anymore. Most teens are so afraid of losing friends that the least little thing can make them feel someone doesn't like them. Your friend could also have had another reason for being upset—anything from a bad test grade to a fight at home. Or your friend may simply have been annoyed because you didn't keep your end of what was agreed on and wear the shirt.

When my friend made such a big deal about it, I thought about lying and saying that my shirt was in the dirty clothes.

Then you would have been telling a social lie. Many people tell social lies when they make E choices, but they do it for different reasons. Three of the main reasons are:

- To avoid hurting someone's feelings. They may also try to make others feel good by what they believe is harmlessly stretching the truth.

- To gain approval. They try to make themselves feel good and look good in the sight of others by embellishing what they are saying.

- To make a more exciting story. They consider not being completely truthful a game.

Some people seldom tell untruths about anything, large or small. They feel that lying is always wrong. On the other hand, they may be so honest that they hurt feelings, sometimes without even realizing they're doing so.

If you choose to tell a social lie when you change your mind about an E choice, realize that this kind of lying can be tricky. Not telling the truth may cause more problems than admitting you made an unpopular choice that others don't like. If your friends find out you lied, they may make a choice about you, a choice you probably won't feel good about. Only you can decide if a social lie is acceptable when an E choice is involved. (With most M and H choices, telling a lie is usually downright dishonest and can cause you serious problems.)

Sometimes you can't hide a bad E choice with a lie. What could I have done the time I wore jeans to a costume party, thinking it would be fine, only to feel like a jerk when I got there and saw everyone else in their costumes? I *really* felt stupid.

You could have gone into the bathroom, combed your hair funny, put your shirt on backward, painted your face with ketchup from the kitchen (if your host said it was okay), and gone back out and enjoyed the party.

Someone would have been sure to make a smart crack if I had done something weird like that.

Sometimes when you make a poor choice, you have a new choice to make. You can stand around and be miserable and let what others say get to you. Or you can tell yourself, I came to enjoy this party, and I can enjoy it if I want to. Remember, only you can control your feelings. Other people can try to make you feel unhappy, but your feelings are your own.

When I do something dumb, I try to tell myself I don't care, but that isn't easy for me to do.

As you begin to grow up, make more of your own choices, and experience more of life, you'll find that you make more poor choices—E, M, and H ones—than you would like. Unfortunately, everyone does, and, as they say, we're all entitled to make our own mistakes.

Living with a mistake is probably easier for some types than others, although it isn't easy, even with an E choice—for anyone in their teen years. Unless they think someone's feelings are hurt, People Persons usually cope with a mistake and Free-and-Fearless tend to move on to new challenges. Sane-and-Sensibles and Considering-and-Carefuls often have the most trouble accepting mistakes they've made. If you are the kind of person who wants to do everything right, you may have a harder time living down a mistake than the person who by temperament lives for the moment and moves on easily from disappointments. Perhaps understanding that trait in yourself and knowing you share it with many others of your type may help you live with a poor choice more easily.

Realize also that you have more choices than you may think and can change some of the choices you've made.

What about changing my mind on an M or H choice?

Just as you should take more time to make an M or H choice, you should take your time when you consider changing your mind about something pretty important. Be sure you are doing the right thing. Go through the four steps of picturing the possibilities several times before deciding to change your mind (see chapter 4). If you do choose to change your choice, you owe it to all the other people who will be affected by your decision to explain very carefully, *with no social lies*, why you've changed your mind and what you are going to do.

Suppose they don't like it and get mad at me?

That happens. Since they were affected by your original choice, they are affected by your change and may not like it. Just because you explain why you changed your mind doesn't mean other people will always agree with either your explanation or your changed plans.

Last year I talked a couple of friends into going to summer camp with me. A week later, my aunt offered to hire me at her store for the summer. I needed the money, so I said sure. I kept waiting for the right time to tell my friends I wasn't going. When I finally did tell them, it was too late for them to get their money back and they had to go on to camp. Wow, were they mad at me!

And with good reason! You changed your choice, but then didn't give them a chance to change theirs. Telling them sooner, however hard that may have been, would have been a better choice. It would have taken into consideration the options of your friends.

They said I ought to go to the camp with them anyway. For a while I thought maybe I should go with them or they might stay mad at me.

Don't stick with an M or H choice simply to protect someone else's feelings. You were right not to make a choice you didn't want because you didn't believe it was in your best interest. Your mistake was that you didn't tell your friends right away. You ended up making them angry because you waited until it was too late for them to change their plans.

When you change an important choice, you have to be willing and able to follow through, to take action that lets others who will be affected by your choice know what is going to happen.

What could I have said to them? One reason I waited so long was because I couldn't think how to say I'd changed my mind.

When you change your mind about something that affects others, try to think of a way to say it that lets both you and the other person save face. You might have said something like this to each friend:

> *I've got good news and bad news. The good news is that my aunt has asked me to work at her store. That means I can make a lot of money. The bad news is that if you decide to go on to camp without me, I'll really miss you. I just hope you don't stay mad at me for changing my mind after I pushed you so hard to sign up for camp.*

If you had let your friends know that you had good reasons for changing your mind and that you understood their feelings, you would have done all that you needed to do.

Did it turn out that you made the better choice?

I guess so. I had lots of fun, but I didn't make as much money as I expected. My cousin decided to work at the store, too, and I had to split the work and the money with him. So I found some odd jobs around the neighborhood to earn extra money.

Making the choice to look elsewhere for the money was a good one. The important thing is not to panic when you find yourself facing the unforeseen. Simply stop and check to see if there are any changes you can make.

If you can't change the outcome, such as not making the amount of money you expected, you might have to find a way to live with the choice you made. People who try to understand why they made a bad choice stand a better chance of making good choices in the future.

▶ *Now, read the following reasons that people can make bad choices. Then, make up examples to go along with each of the reasons listed. For example, make up a situation in which someone made a choice because they wanted to do what their friends were doing. When you're done, we'll talk some more about what you can do when you decide to change your mind about a choice.*

Why Anyone Can Make a Bad Choice

1. **Lydia is careless in picturing the possibilities and doesn't really think through all the things that might happen as a result of her choice.** Next time she needs to remind herself to think before she acts.

   Now think of an example of this kind of choice.

2. **Alan saw that something bad might happen, but he wanted to go along with his friends more than he was worried about the consequences of his choice.** If something bad does happen, he has to ask himself, Was it worth it?

   Now think of an example of this kind of choice.

3. **Sydney felt daring.** She felt that nothing could possibly happen to her. Maybe she felt she'd never get caught. In fact, bad things can happen to her and she can get caught.

   Now think of an example of this kind of choice.

4. **Lars did it to get attention from someone.** There are better ways of getting attention than doing something foolish. Besides, why did he need the attention? He should think about that first and do something constructive about his problems. He needs to talk to his counselor or an adult he feels close to and can trust.

   Now think of an example of this kind of choice.

5. **Min was bored.** Doing something was better than doing nothing and being bored. What else could she have done instead of what she chose to do? Does she need something new and interesting in her life like a hobby or a new friend or a new skill?

   Now think of an example of this kind of choice.

6. **Raoul felt depressed and didn't care what happened.** That's a bad state of affairs. He should do something about feeling depressed right away. He shouldn't take any chances. He needs to talk to his parents, doctor, clergy, counselor, or teacher. He shouldn't gamble with his life.

   Now think of an example of this kind of choice.

7. **Jillian's choice was a risk, but she felt lucky.** Luck is just that—luck. It has a way of running out. She shouldn't take unnecessary chances.

   Now think of an example of this kind of choice.

8. **Rob wanted to get even with someone.** Getting even often means either getting hurt or making matters worse. He should try to deal with why he and the other person aren't getting along rather than trying to get even.

   Now think of an example of this kind of choice.

But what if it was a really, truly bad choice like one my friend made? He skipped school and went to the mall. Then he saw his mom headed toward him and slipped and broke his arm when he tried to run up the down escalator. Before the whole thing was over, he was in all kinds of trouble at home and at school.

That's certainly a good example of doing all the wrong things after making a bad choice. The moment you realize you have made a bad choice, do two things:

- Avoid making matters worse.

- Do what you can to make things right.

What do you mean by "avoid making matters worse"?

When you realize that you have done something wrong, you can choose to face up to your behavior or to run away from it. When you try to pretend you didn't do anything wrong (or, like your friend, to outrun being caught), you end up making matters worse for yourself. Your friend should have owned up to skipping school and taken his punishment. He wouldn't have gone through the pain of a broken arm and the extra upset to his mom.

What could he have said?

He could simply have said, "Mom, you caught me. I'm sorry. I know I shouldn't be skipping school, but I did." That would have given his mom a chance to work with him instead of against him.

But I bet she still would have punished him and so would the principal.

Probably. We're not saying that by cooperating you will avoid punishment, but people are less likely to give a harsh punishment to people who act sorry for what they did and own up to it. Accept your responsibility for making a bad choice. When you are wrong, don't make the situation worse by adding more bad choices to the original one.

That makes sense, but how is trying to make things right different from taking responsibility for what you did?

For example, if you borrow a sweater from someone and splash paint on it, you not only admit you did it and say you are sorry, you have the sweater cleaned or replace it. You have to make matters right or risk long-term problems of hard feelings with the other person.

My mom is always saying I have to change and start taking more responsibility for what I do. I guess she's right.

Change is the key word for being a teen. And changes affect your choices. So let's talk about change and how you can deal with it.

> ▶ *Take a few moments now to think about what you can do when you change your mind about a choice you've made. The following scenarios will help you think about how to go about changing your plans. Try to put yourself in the place of the person making the decision, then choose what you think is the best choice for that person. Then we'll talk about a different kind of change you can make—a change to yourself.*

Who's the Joke On?

Gabriella was sure she would hate Ms. Lafayette, the new science teacher. No one could take the place of Mr. Kelly. So when Ms. LaFayette asked students to tell her the names they preferred to be called, Gabriella decided to play a trick.

"Call me Maria," she said. At lunch, when her classmates questioned her, Gabriella told them, "Well, my first name *is* Maria, even if no one ever calls me that. Besides, it's a good joke to play on her."

Every time Ms. LaFayette called her Maria, a few snickers sounded across the room. And after class Gabriella felt smug when she heard students laughing about her joke and "how stupid" Ms. LaFayette was not to pick up on the name change.

Within a few weeks, though, the students discovered that Ms. Lafayette liked and cared about them and actually made science fun. Gabriella, too, began to like Ms. LaFayette, but she couldn't figure out how she could stop the joke now without looking foolish.

One day when Gabriella was shopping with her mother, she spied Ms. LaFayette walking toward the checkout where she and her mother waited in line.

"Hello," said Ms. LaFayette. "You must be Ms. Augustina," she said to Gabriella's mom. "I'm so glad to meet you. I've been wanting to tell you what a good student Gabriella is." Ms. LaFayette turned to Gabriella. "I can call you Gabriella outside of class, can't I?" she asked with a smile.

Things to Consider

- Do you think Gabriella made the right choice when she decided to trick Ms. LaFayette?

- Did she make the right choice by continuing the trick?

- What choices does Gabriella have now?

- What would you do if you were Gabriella?

The Shakedown

Ricky was nervous. He hated going to a new school. He thought he'd get along all right with the teachers, but, because he was shy, he dreaded meeting new kids. Now, as the bell rang to signal the end of morning classes and lunch break, he knew he would have to deal with a noisy, crowded lunchroom. He brushed his hair off his forehead with his hand and tucked his books under his arm. Might as well hit the restroom, he thought. That will use up at least a few minutes before I have to face the cafeteria line and find someone to sit with during lunch.

He found a door labeled BOYS over the door and ducked in. Suddenly he realized he was in the midst of four older students. They glared at him. "Hey, I bet he can help us out. Got any money for lunch?" the biggest kid said to Ricky. "Yeah, you don't want us to go hungry, do you?" laughed another.

Ricky knew his mom was expecting change from the $5 bill she had thrust in his hand that morning as he ran for the bus. He quickly thought of his choices as he looked at the boys.

Their eyes were on him. Maybe if he gave them the money, they would leave him alone. He hesitated a second and then slowly withdrew the bill from his jeans pocket.

"And don't tell anyone about this *loan*," one of the boys said as they walked toward the door. "Or you'll be sorry."

Ricky breathed a sigh of relief. Even if he didn't have anything to eat today and would have to lie to his mom about what happened to her money, at least the kids were gone and his problem was hopefully solved.

Things to Consider

- Do you think Ricky made the right choice?

- What do you think will happen in the future between Ricky and the four boys?

- If you were Ricky, what would you have done when the boys confronted you?

- What choices would you make now if you were Ricky?

How About Helping Me Out?

Sol pulled Jackson aside. "How about helping me out?" he said. "You never get in any trouble."

The last comment made Jackson feel a little uneasy. Despite his reservations, he said, "Sure, if I can." He meant it, because Sol hardly ever talked to him, even though Jackson certainly wanted to be in the in-group of kids that considered Sol their leader.

"Walk this way with me," Sol said.

Jackson hoped some of the kids noticed as he and Sol made their way through the crowded hall. As they walked, Sol reached in his pocket and pulled out a brown paper bag. "Just stick this in your pocket till last period," he said.

Jackson knew this was not the time to ask questions. He quickly jammed the bag in his jacket pocket and headed for the cafeteria. Sol just as quickly disappeared into the crush of students.

Jackson felt pleased with himself as he got in the lunch line behind his music teacher, Mrs. Cohen, and a substitute teacher. Suddenly his stomach turned over as he heard the substitute say, "I heard in the lounge that some students at school have firecrackers and are planning to explode them in toilets."

"Don't worry," said Mrs. Cohen. "The administration knows, and Ms. Myers is great at tracking down kids involved in that kind of thing and making them sorry they ever considered a prank like that."

Things to Consider

- Do you think Jackson made the right choice?

- What would you have done if you were Jackson and Sol asked you for help?

- What choices does Jackson have now?

- What do you think will happen?

- What would you choose to do if you were Jackson?

8

Choosing to Change

Your *older sister:*	I don't see what the big deal is. It's my life and my choice! And it's not as if I'm going to look like a freak or something!
Your mom:	Well, I think you will! You simply cannot have your nose pierced the week before your cousin's wedding. What will our relatives say? I've always bragged about what a sensible young woman you are. I'll never forgive you. If I weren't so angry about this, I'd cry.
You:	I just love listening to my sister and mom deal with their choices!

We've talked a lot about choices you can control, but things are also happening to you over which you have no control. You see and sense that all kinds of physical and emotional changes are taking place as you move through adolescence. Some of these changes happen earlier for some kids and later for others, but sooner or later they happen to everyone. Such surges of growth and hormones (and the feelings that go along with them) are normal changes over which you have little choice but to adapt.

Because of these changes, many young people choose this time in their lives to make changes in other aspects of their lives—everything from how they look to how they spend their time. Choosing to change is a way of taking more control of their lives.

I guess the changes are what cause my mom to look at me and say stuff like, "Oh, you're growing up so fast!" whenever I want to do something new or different.

Parents say that kind of thing both because they see changes in you and because they realize they are changing, too, and growing older. Both things are scary for the adults who are responsible for you. In many ways, it's hard for them to watch you grow up.

But I want to grow up!

And you will, for sure, although maybe not as fast as you would sometimes like. Your parents may wish they could hold you back because they know that the physical changes that are happening set in motion other social and emotional changes.

Sometimes I think I'd like to change everything in my life.

Don't try to change everything in your life all at once. For starters, why not pick out a couple of small ways to change—some E or M choices, perhaps.

I think I'd really like to change my hair.

Why would you like to change it?

Well, I don't want to look like a little kid anymore. I also want to look more like my friends, and I guess a part of me just wants to show my dad. He's always telling me how to cut my hair.

You've given the three main reasons people your age often have for choosing to change:

- You want to make a statement about who you are.

- You want to go along with your friends.

- You want to rebel against somebody or something.

Since these can be either good reasons or bad reasons for change, depending on the situation, you should picture the possibilities before choosing to make changes.

What could be bad about changing my hair?

There's nothing wrong with changing your hairstyle. Since hair does grow out, you probably will have to live with a bad choice only a couple of months. A few months, however, can seem like a very long time indeed at this stage of your life, especially if the hairstyle to die for this month suddenly seems totally horrible next month.

▶ *Now, before reading on, take a few moments to read the following situation that involves consideration of personal change and appearance. Try to put yourself in the place of the person in the story, then decide what you think would be the best choice for that person. Then we'll talk a bit more about making personal changes.*

Curly Top

Tony couldn't believe it. All these years he had worn a crew cut and brushed his hand over it whenever he talked to the guys. Now, all of a sudden, his hair had started coming out curly! Not just a bit of a wave, but sissy, girlie curly. His brother teased him and told him he was getting "pretty." His mom twirled his curls with her fingers and told him that he had little golden ducktails all over his head when he was a baby. His dad just grunted and told him to keep it cut short like the Marine he wanted him to be some day. But Marika, beautiful, ever-so-cool, Marika loved it!

"Please let it grow long," she begged Tony.

So he did. In about two months, he didn't look like himself when he looked in the mirror and Marika couldn't keep her hands out of his hair. One month later, Tony was staring at himself in the mirror, when his dad stopped to talk to him.

"I want you to get that mop cut. I'm ashamed to be seen with you looking like some freak," said his dad.

Tony's Choices: What Should He Do?

(a) Tuck his hair up under a cap when around his dad.

(b) Shave his head. If he was supposed to look like a Marine, that would show his dad.

(c) Get his hair cut just enough to get his dad off his back.

(d) Pay no attention to his dad. If Marika liked his hair, that was the most important thing, and Mom would keep Dad from blowing his top.

(e) He could dye his hair the school colors—bright green with a streak of blue down the middle. That would show his dad whose hair it was!

(f) What other choices could Tony make?

I guess even more than hair, I'd like to change my weight.

That's a far more serious choice than changing hairstyle. With something like weight, it's important to understand the difference between the way you feel you look and a medical reality—like actually being overweight. If your concern about your weight is based on a medical reality, then follow the suggestions here, but if it's more a matter of how you feel, then think about why you feel that way and talk to your friends and parents about how they see you. You might discover that they see you quite differently from the way you see yourself. They may disagree with you and think your weight is just right for you. Also, if your doctor tells you that your weight is just right, take his or her word for it.

If you do determine that there is a need to adjust your weight, then think about your plans carefully. If you don't choose a way that is good for your body when you try to change your weight or your muscle structure, your choice can hurt you for the rest of your life. Any choices that affect you for years to come or perhaps for your lifetime are truly H choices that require special care as you picture the possibilities.

Make yourself a promise that *before* you choose to make any major H choice about changing the way you look, you will go through these steps:

- Take your type into account

- Read the current medical advice on the subject

- Picture the possibilities with at least one adult you trust

- Plan carefully how you will go about making the change

How can thinking about my type help me?

Why you want to change and how you go about making that change depends a lot on your type.

If you are a People Person, you might choose to do something because your friends are doing it and you think they will like you better if you do it, too. That's how you can end up with green hair with split ends, a horrible looking jacket that eats up all of your allowance, or something worse. When you are tempted to make a choice for change, think about your *own* values. Ask yourself if it is something that you yourself really want. Don't let anyone rush you into a decision. There are other ways to get people to like you besides making a choice that is not in your own best interest.

If you are Sane-and-Sensible, you are not too likely to make any choice on the spur of the moment. You probably choose to change only because you see a good reason to do so. But don't be so sane and sensible that if everyone in your class is buying purple socks, you don't do it because you're afraid that their color might run onto your white socks when you wash them. Choosing to be one of the crowd on something small like that, basically an E choice, is just part of being sociable. For M and H choices, consider your own best interest after you look at facts, feelings, and outcomes.

If you are Free-and-Fearless, be extra careful about how you choose. The idea to do something crazy may shoot into your head and you may do it without thinking about the outcome or long-term effects. That's how people end up wearing chain-covered jeans to their sister's formal wedding—or getting tattoos or having their nose pierced, only to find that they regret it five years later. Before you do something drastic, make yourself a promise that when you choose to do anything with effects that last longer than a month, you'll wait twenty-four hours before you do it and that you'll slow down and follow all four of the steps we listed earlier for making H choices.

If you are Considering-and-Careful, go with that feeling in the pit of your stomach. Most of the time, it will lead you to make good choices. Don't let someone talk you into choosing to do something that you know doesn't feel right. You, of all people, will hate yourself if you make a bad choice and have to live with it for months or even years to come.

After you consider your type, make a trek to the library. The librarian can help you locate reliable information you'll need to consider before you can make a good choice. The librarian may also be a person who can help you picture the possibilities of your choices more fully.

I get along okay with the school librarian, but I'd never ask her for help with a hard choice. I just don't think she'd understand me.

Maybe she wouldn't, but we bet you can find someone who will give you unbiased opinions and ideas. Don't begin making an H change happen without talking it over first with some adult—preferably a parent—who will talk candidly and fairly with you.

If your choice still seems like a good idea after you talk it over with an adult, plan carefully how you will carry out the change you want. How much will this new you cost? Where will you get the money to make this change? Does your change require the help of others? Can anything go wrong with your choice that planning can prevent?

I may never make a change in myself if I do all that. You make everything sound like school. Read this, learn that. I already have to learn so much junk in school—stuff I'll never need—that I don't feel like going out and learning more stuff.

As you go through your teen years, you will surely learn lots of things you'll never use. We won't argue with you on that point.

But look at learning another way: Think of ideas and information as the ingredients that go into the recipe for your life. If you have only flour and water and yeast in a kitchen, you can make bread, but it will be pretty plain bread, with little aroma and less flavor. On the other hand, in a kitchen filled with all kinds of ingredients, you can make lots of wonderful things that are great to sniff and look at, and with flavors that are wonderful to taste.

So it is with what you learn. If you are willing to learn only a few things, you'll live a very restricted life. But the more you learn, the more you can learn, and the more choices you have about what you want to do or be as you get older. Just as you like some dishes now that you didn't care for as a little kid, some ideas and facts that seem useless or boring now can turn out to be important ingredients of your life in years to come as changes take place. The science experiment that seems pointless now may spark an interest that eventually helps guide your career choice. The foreign language you hate to study may help you have a fantastic trip abroad.

There is no way to know which ingredients will flavor your future, so, if you're smart, you'll choose to learn as much as you can about everything now.

I guess there's some sense in what you say. This year I decided I wanted to take tennis lessons just to see if I could learn to play the game. At first I had to practice all kinds of things that didn't seem to matter, like paying attention to my footwork, turning quickly, and always keeping my eye on the ball. But as I got better, I found that they did.

Just so. By the way, learning a new sport is a great way to find out more about who you are and what you like—both key to making decisions that will matter a great deal in the future.

Don't forget that you may also want to learn some new social skills along with some new physical skills. Learning how to come across as a person who is self-confident yet sensitive to another person's point of view is a major social skill that many teens have never learned.

I never thought of learning how to get along with others as a skill like skating or playing the piano.

In many areas there are even classes you can take in such things as formal manners, how to dress, or how to make speeches. Check with your librarian or counselor for other possibilities in your community.

Right now I'd like to try out for the swim team because my best friend is on the team, but I'm not a very fast swimmer. I'm scared I'll get a cramp in my leg and never be able to help the team in the relay. And my coordination seems weird lately, anyway.

Take into account that while your body is changing, you may actually *be* clumsier at anything physical for a while, but as you get adjusted to your new, more grown-up body, being awkward will fade away.

For some types, making mistakes when first learning a new skill is especially worrisome. But try to realize that nearly everyone has to struggle to learn new things. If you finally decide the new sport or skill is just not your thing and you can't learn it well or don't enjoy it, then relax, give it up, and take aim at another choice.

You make choosing changes in my life sound like a game of trying to make a basket or hit a target.

At your age, choosing to change is very much like trying to hit a target. You're at the stage of life when trying new things, aiming at new targets, is a great idea.

Try actually writing down some targets that you want to aim for in the next month, school quarter, and year. You could write them out and put them on your mirror or on the front page of your notebook.

▶ *Take a few moments now to get started with your goal setting by doing the exercise on the following page. When you're done, we'll talk some more about setting goals and planning changes.*

Goals to Aim For

In I Week

In I Month

In I Year

You mean things like making a better grade in math or joining the swim team or trying out for student government?

Or getting along better with your parents or even being better friends with your kid brother. You might try putting targets on your computer so they pop up on the screen when you boot up. If your targets are someplace where you're reminded of them, you are more likely to remember to work at choosing new and different ways that can lead to a new and different you.

If you try to do too many things, you may not be able to do any one of them very well. So choose no more than three things to check out in the next few months.

Now, why don't you make one more choice this very minute? Choose to have a great day today. Picture the possibility of having some fun, doing some neat things.

That's a great choice. And it's not even an M or H one. It's an E choice for sure. I'm on my way!

9

Using Choosing

"I've decided to buy a blue sweater."

"Dad, I have to study for a test tomorrow, so I can't go to Gram's then, but you can count on my going Tuesday."

"No, thanks, I don't want a cigarette. Why?
It's just not my thing."

"Mom, I know you'd like me to keep on taking music,
but I want to take tennis lessons instead. Here's why."

Are these statements the "new you" talking now that you have learned about making choices? Here are some additional tips to help you get better control over your life not only now that you're a teenager, but also in the years ahead:

- Learn to size up a choice as being an E, M, or H one before you take action. Often a situation that seems terribly important—an H at first glance—is really only an E, or at most an M, when you look closely. You'll be nothing but a mess of stress if you treat every decision as an H one!

- If you treat every choice as an H one, you will probably find that parents and teachers won't respect you. They will think you don't know what is important or how to set priorities.

- Think before you speak when trying to persuade parents to go along with your choice. If you have a major tantrum every time you discuss an E choice that they disagree with, they won't take your emotions seriously when a real H choice is at stake. Slamming a door never makes anyone respect your decision.

- Never forget what a great resource parents are when you make choices. They may not be able to program a VCR, but they can give you good advice on getting along with other people and making value choices. Many problems don't change through the years. Your mom and dad have lived through boy-girl problems, fights with friends, and lone-liness and blues, too. They really can help you picture the possibilities.

- Picturing the possibilities often leaves you with two or more good solutions. You may often find no one choice that is clearly better than another. Choosing to take tennis lessons rather than music lessons is not better or worse, just differ-ent. Each will lead you along a different path. So once you choose, don't look back and dwell on the choice you didn't make, but do everything you can to make the one you did choose work out right for you.

- If you sincerely try to make a choice work and find later it was a bad one, analyze what further choices you now have available. Take action and move on with your life in a positive way.

- If you choose to make a choice that is unpopular with friends, you may find yourself standing alone. Standing alone isn't easy or comfortable, but if it is the right choice for you, stick with it.

- Finally, you are what you choose. The clothes you choose, the actions you choose, the studies you choose, the friends you choose—all shape you. They structure your life, tell people who you are. So make the best choices you can.

Choose a *good* life for yourself. You deserve it.

Selected Resources

Farris, D. *Type Tales*. 1990. Palo Alto, CA: Consulting Psychologists Press.

Giovannoni, L., L. V. Berens, and S. A. Cooper. 1988. *Introduction to Temperament*. Huntington Beach, CA: Telos Publications.

Lawrence, G. 1993. *People Types and Tiger Stripes*. 3d ed. Gainesville, FL: Center for Applications of Psychological Type, Inc.

Madaras, L. 1987. *What's Happening to My Body?: For Boys*. New York: Newmarket Press.

Madaras, L. 1987. *What's Happening to My Body?: For Girls*. New York: Newmarket Press.

Wirths, C. G., and M. Bowman-Kruhm. 1992. *Are You My Type? Or Why Aren't You More Like Me?* Palo Alto, CA: Consulting Psychologists Press.